Insider Trading

Learn Amerca's dirty secrets
and
history behind Wall Street

Jason Rockwell

INSIDER TRADING

America's dirty secrets and history behind Wall Street

Contents

1. Introduction 4
    1.1 Relevance 5
2. What is Insider trading? 7
3. Effects of Insider trading 9
    3.1 Spin security prices 9
    3.2 Reduced Trust in the System 10
    3.3 Reduced trust in the company 10
4. Tracking Insider Trading 11
    4.1 Tipping 11
    4.2 Hacking 11
5. US Insider Trading Laws 11
    5.1 Form 4 12
    5.2 Rule 10b5 12
    5.3 Rule 10b5-1 Plans 12
    5.4 Sarbanes-Oxley Act, 2002 13
    5.5 Misappropriation theory 13
    5.6 Rule 14e-3 14
    5.7 Stop Trading on Congressional Knowledge (STOCK) Act 14
6. Landmark cases 15
7. Recent insider trading cases 18
8. Should insider trading be legal? 20
9. Steps to check insider trading 22
10. Conclusion 23
11. References 24

1. Introduction

February, 1995, one of world's oldest merchant bank collapsed with losses worth £862MN (economic value ~ £2,052MN today) caused by one person and his greed – Nick Leeson.

A 28 years old employee brought down 233-year-old Barings bank within 6 years of joining the bank. In the short duration, he made unauthorized speculative trades and earned the bank almost 10% of its annual profits. He built the reputation of a market mover and was soon elevated to the position of chief trader and head of settlements at Barings Singapore branch. This gave him free control over all transactions. He used it for hiding his losses in an old error account 88888.

On official books his trades were always profitable while he fished away losses worth almost £380MN under account 88888 till 1994.

Losses deepened as his bet on Nikkei failed. 16 January 1995, he placed a short term straddle betting that the Japanese Stock market, Nikkei would not move significantly overnight. Though, this was one of his safer bets, as luck would have it, Kobe earthquake hit early in the morning, the next day and markets plummeted. Nick suffered huge losses on that trade. Led by panic and greed to quickly recover these losses, he bet again on quick recovery of Nikkei. But markets kept falling, deepening his losses. By the time, the incident was brought to light, Barings losses had increased to £2.2BN, much higher than the banks' capital and reserves put together. The bank collapsed under the burden of such huge losses and left lessons to be learnt.

Nick Leeson almost 50 today, feels that neither banks nor traders have learnt from the incident. History has been repeating itself with the recent crisis as one the biggest example of bankers driven by greed for money and power.

1.1 Relevance

The white collar crime; insider trading has blackened some of the biggest names of the financial world and brought down some of the biggest institutions causing huge losses to economies and public savings. This book explains insider trading; its effects on security prices and the evolution of laws and regulatory institutions around it.

Rockwell, provides a unique understanding of insider trading from a trader, an investor and a regulators' perspective. 'Greed in the end fails even the greedy'- Cathryn Louis. The biggest of names have come down because of insider trading, yet more and more cases of insider trading are coming to light. Given this, the authors' compilation is a great read. After reading the book, you would have known about the following: -

- What is insider trading?
- Effects of insider trading
- US insider trading laws
- Landmark cases and recent cases
- Should insider trading be made legal?
- Steps to Check insider trading

Enjoy reading, Enjoy Learning!

© **Copyright 2014 by A Touch of Wisdom - All rights reserved.**

This document is geared towards providing exact and reliable information in regards to the topic and issue covered. The publication is sold with the idea that the publisher is not required to render accounting, officially permitted, or otherwise, qualified services. If advice is necessary, legal or professional, a practiced individual in the profession should be ordered.

- From a Declaration of Principles which was accepted and approved equally by a Committee of the American Bar Association and a Committee of Publishers and Associations.

In no way is it legal to reproduce, duplicate, or transmit any part of this document in either electronic means or in printed format. Recording of this publication is strictly prohibited and any storage of this document is not allowed unless with written permission from the publisher. All rights reserved.

The information provided herein is stated to be truthful and consistent, in that any liability, in terms of inattention or otherwise, by any usage or abuse of any policies, processes, or directions contained within is the solitary and utter responsibility of the recipient reader. Under no circumstances will any legal responsibility or blame be held against the publisher for any reparation, damages, or monetary loss due to the information herein, either directly or indirectly.

Respective authors own all copyrights not held by the publisher.

The information herein is offered for informational purposes solely, and is universal as so. The presentation of the information is without contract or any type of guarantee assurance.

The trademarks that are used are without any consent, and the publication of the trademark is without permission or backing by the trademark owner. All trademarks and brands within this book are for clarifying purposes only and are the owned by the owners themselves, not affiliated with this document.

2. What is Insider trading?

Is it someone trading inside a room? Or a person inside a company trading?

It is both. In simple terms, insider trading is when a person inside a company makes trades with additional information that has not yet left the room i.e. he has access to additional information by virtue of his position, that is not available to others.

An insider is defined as an officer, director or owner of 10% or more of a class of shares in a corporation. This includes not only executives working for companies, but also other entities such as mutual funds, hedge funds or institutions that hold an amount equal to or greater than 10% of issued and outstanding shares.

SEC explains that insider trading includes both legal and illegal conduct. It is legal when corporate insiders - officers, directors, and employees; buy and sell stock in their own companies. When corporate insiders trade in their own securities, they must report their trades to the SEC.

Illegal insider trading is buying or selling a security, in breach of a fiduciary duty or other relationship of trust and confidence, while in possession of material, nonpublic information about the security. Insider trading violations may also include tipping such information, securities trading by the person tipped and securities trading by those who misappropriate such information.

For example, illegal insider trading would occur if the CEO of Company A learned, prior to a public announcement, that Company A will be taken over and then bought shares in Company A knowing that the share price would likely rise.

In an illegal insider trading, an insider in a company buys the stock, shares price-sensitive information with a small group of people who buy the stocks and spread the word. Soon a huge artificial demand is created for the particular stock resulting in higher prices. At a certain point when the prices hit the satisfactory level the insider exits along with his small group of people or in other words sells the stocks and make profits. Soon the stocks plummet resulting in huge losses for the public investors.

Though most operations in the stock market, various factors do cause people to fall by the wayside. Extreme circumstances like the recent financial crisis and recession could prompt someone to resort to insider trading. Also with more alpha men and women, more people tend to bend the rules for the high stakes at hand. Conflicting rules and incentives promote insider trading, too. Although it's illegal to trade on material nonpublic information, professional investors may be more apt to because their pay is usually tied to performance. That can make the temptation to use inside information irresistible, especially now that the financial markets are larger and more competitive than ever. Insider trading isn't always about success, money and greed, though. It can also result from simple negligence where an employee inadvertently reveals confidential information about a company to an outsider, who then succumbs to the temptation to act on the information.

Insider trading can undermine investor confidence in the fairness and integrity of the securities markets. The SEC therefore treats the detection and prosecution of insider trading violations as one of its enforcement priorities.

3. Effects of Insider trading

Insider trading impacts both the markets and the market sentiment in the following ways:

3.1 Spin security prices

Insiders usually own significant stake in a company. Trades made by them can therefore significantly move the security prices given the trade value they can generate. When such trades are driven by information not available to a greater public, it places insiders in an advantageous position which, when exploited can cause huge losses to other market participants.

Illustration

Day 1: The Chairman of Company B, by virtue of his position knows that the company is going to face some legal battles for past actions and this negative news once public will cause Company B shares to plummet. He owns 8% in the company. Let us now compare this with the trade of one retail investor who owns less than 0.000001% stake in a company. He is not aware of this information as it is not yet public. The share of Company B has been doing well and he expects the security price to rise further. Basis this he invests some hard earned money into the markets. Another 10,000 such investors buy the stock with the expectation of making profits.

Day 2: Before the information becomes public, to protect his investments, the CFO sells his 8% stake in the company. Even if the 10,000 retail investors buy the stock, the security price will plummet as the CFO controls 8% of the value whereas the retail investors collectively also own less than 1% in the company. Once the CFO makes a sale, market will panic on that stock, knowing that something is wrong and will trigger a panic sale sending the stock price in distress.

Insiders may directly sell their stock or tip off the information to family and friends to protect personal interests. Similarly, a reverse situation where stock prices are expected to rise, insiders may buy at lower prices and make huge profits.

Such trades can produce major shifts in a stock's price. Other investors may notice this and overreact, causing even more price volatility. The confusion and volatility may spread to similar stocks or even the overall stock market.

3.2 Reduced Trust in the System

Fair and efficient stock market operations depend on all investors having the same access to information about publicly traded companies. When investors act on inside information before it becomes widely available, they get an unfair advantage that shakes peoples' trust in the financial system and economy. An insider trade may cause the retail investors to sell at low prices or make them buy at higher prices, eating into their profits. Such acts of insider trading discourage small investors from participating in the market and reduce it to a betting platform than a source for raising funds. Trust is implicit in this arrangement between a company and its investors. The corporation's officers are supposed to act in the best interest of the company's shareholders. Insider trading is a betrayal of that trust; by acting on information that shareholders aren't privy to for financial gain, officers of a corporation are acting purely in their own best interests.

When entire markets are widely perceived to be tainted by insider trading, average people who are also potential investors avoid markets altogether. Prior to the 1990s, when the European Economic Community made its member states adopt measures to combat illegal insider trading, the common perception among Europeans was that their markets were rife with insider trading. As a result, Europe saw its markets increase in value and trading activity after anti-insider trading policies spread.

3.3 Reduced trust in the company

Significant shifts in a company stock can be traced to public announcements, changes in the economy or company performance reports. But when a stock fluctuates for no apparent reason; like it might with insider trading, public may lose confidence in the company and fewer people would be willing to invest in it or buy its products or services. This can also make it difficult for a accompany to raise funds in the market in the future.

Insider trading can hurt people financially and emotionally. Short term traders can easily lose money in a stock that becomes very volatile due to insider trades. If an insider trading scandal damages a company's finances or reputation enough, long-term shareholders might lose money as a result of an extended drop in the firm's stock. Allowing insider trading to go unchecked could hurt confidence in the system enough to hinder the economy in general.

4. Tracking Insider Trading

Though many cases keep coming to light on insider trading, it happens only when the market has already incurred huge losses. Such cases are few. Big trades like those done directly by the top executives can be identified smaller trades, tipping and hacking which are all very difficult to trace.

4.1 Tipping

An insider may not directly be involved in an illegal trade but may part with valuable insider information. This is called tipping. It is difficult to identify and prove trades led by tipping yet a number of cases have been brought to light. One of most recent high profile case is that of Golfer Phil Mickelson who has been fined for $1Mn for profits he made on an insider stock tip. The complaint sites that Phil owed money to his gambler friend Walters. Walters had insider information from his friend Davis, former Chairman of Dean foods on an upcoming spin off planned by the company. Phil bought the stock on Walters's advice and sold it at a profit of $0.9MN. In this case, powerful names make money by virtue of their position leaving less informed retail investors to absorb the losses.

4.2 Hacking

Wire frauds are becoming common day by day and are difficult to control. Hacking into company's critical databases and reports reveals the insider information to the hackers. They further use it to trade in the company's stocks making profits. One of the recent cases is where Alexander Garkusha, accused of a $100MN insider trading scheme plead guilty of committing a wire fraud.

Also, proving that someone has been responsible for a trade can be difficult because traders may try to hide behind nominees, offshore companies, and other proxies. The Securities and Exchange Commission, SEC prosecutes over 50 cases each year, with many being settled administratively out of court. The SEC and several stock exchanges actively monitor trading, looking for suspicious activity. The SEC does not have criminal enforcement authority, but can refer serious matters to the U.S. Attorney's Office for further investigation and prosecution.

5. US Insider Trading Laws

The United States has been the leading country in prohibiting insider trading made on the basis of material non-public information. Insider trading has a base offense level of 8, which puts it in Zone A under the U.S. Sentencing Guidelines. This implies that first-time offenders are eligible to receive probation rather than incarceration. We discuss some of the major disclosure norms and rules used by the US government to check insider trading.

5.1 Form 4

In the United States, trading conducted by corporate officers, key employees, directors, or significant shareholders must be reported to the regulator or publicly disclosed, usually within a few business days of the trade. In these cases, insiders in the United States are required to file a Form 4 with the U.S. Securities and Exchange Commission, SEC when buying or selling shares of their own companies.

5.2 Rule 10b5

The rule 10B-5 codified at 17 C.F.R.240 is a regulation formally known as the Employment of Manipulative and Deceptive Practices that was created under the Securities Exchange Act of 1934. This rule deems it illegal for anybody to directly or indirectly use any measure to defraud, make false statements, omit relevant information or otherwise conduct operations of business that would deceive another person; in relation to conducting transactions involving stock and other securities.

5.3 Rule10b5-1 Plans

An extension of Rule 10b5, this rule was enacted to resolve the unsettled issue over the definition of insider trading which is prohibited under Rule 10b-5. Under Rule 10b5-1, large stockholders, directors, officers and other insiders who regularly possess material nonpublic information (MNPI) but who nonetheless wish to buy or sell stock may establish an affirmative defense to an illegal insider trading charge by adopting a written plan to buy or sell at a time when they are not in possession of MNPI. The plan typically takes the form of a contract between the insider and his or her broker.

The plan must be entered into at a time when the insider has no MNPI about the company or its securities. The plan must:

- 1. specify the amount, price and specific dates of purchases or sales; or
- 2. include a formula or similar method for determining amount, price and date; or
- 3. give the broker the exclusive right to determine whether, how and when to make purchases and sales, as long as the broker does so without being aware of MNPI at the time the trades are made.

Under the first two alternatives, the 10b5-1 plan cannot give the broker any discretion as to trade dates. As a result, a plan that requests the broker to sell 1,000 shares per week would have to meet the requirements under the third alternative. On the other hand, under the second alternative, the date may be specified by indicating that trades should be made on any date on which the limit price is hit.

The affirmative defense is only available if the trade is in fact made pursuant to the preset terms of the 10b5-1 plan (unless the terms are revised at a time when the insider is not aware of any MNPI and could therefore enter into a new plan). Trades are deemed not to have been made pursuant to the plan if the insider later enters into or alters a corresponding or hedging transaction or position with respect to the securities covered by the plan.

5.4 Sarbanes-Oxley Act, 2002

Reporting rules for companies have been toughened by the SEC over time to define more clearly the circumstances under which insiders can trade. In the wake of a number of Wall Street scandals, the U.S. Congress took part in a cleanup effort.

It is hard enough to regain trust when officers of a single company trade illegally. When illegal insider trading encompasses several companies, as the scandal surrounding Enron, its auditors and the entire system of accounting checks and balances did, the broken trust was far-reaching. Following the Enron debacle, Congress enacted the controversial Sarbanes-Oxley Act, 2002 to restore public confidence. This act mandated some powerful changes to reporting requirements. It requires insiders to report trades by the second day following the transaction, rather than the 10th day of the month following the trade as was required under the old rules. The act holds officers directly accountable for any errors, omissions or dishonesty in corporate reporting, is widely believed to have helped public confidence in the markets following the Enron scandal. This reporting requirement goes a long way toward leveling the playing field for retail investors, making insider data a far more effective and timely tool in the process. Between July 31, 2002 and July 31, 2007, the New York Stock Exchange grew 67 percent, about $4.2 trillion

5.5 Misappropriation theory

Misappropriation theory states that anyone who misappropriates information from his or her employer and trades on that information in any stock (either the employer's stock or the company's competitor stocks) may be guilty of insider trading.

For example, if a journalist who worked for Company B learned about the takeover of Company A while performing his work duties and bought stock in Company A, illegal insider trading might still have occurred. Even though the journalist did not violate a fiduciary duty to Company A's shareholders, he might have violated a fiduciary duty to Company B's shareholders (assuming the newspaper had a policy of not allowing reporters to trade on stories they were covering).

The misappropriation theory became the means for the SEC to respond to political pressures from Congress about the abuses from insider trading while avoiding a definition of insider trading that the Commission felt would be used by lawyers to constrict enforcement efforts. Hostile takeovers themselves, argued the SEC, were not the problem, but the abuse of inside information that naturally arose from such takeovers demanded regulation. Ever mindful of its mission to restore public and investor confidence in the markets, the SEC promoted the misappropriation theory as a way to accomplish both goals.

5.6 Rule 14e-3

Congress's failure to directly prohibit trading on material information about hostile takeovers and to define insider trading based on the misappropriation theory altered the SEC legal strategy and led the SEC to administratively adopt Rule 14e-3.

Rule 14e-3 prohibits insiders of the bidder and the target from divulging confidential information about a tender offer, exactly the kind of stock tip information the Supreme Court in *Chiarella* had found not to be a Rule 10b-5 violation. In addition, Rule14e-3, with narrow exceptions, prohibits any person who possesses material information relating to a tender offer by another person from trading in target company securities if the bidder has commenced to taken substantial steps towards commencement of the bid.

5.7 Stop Trading on Congressional Knowledge (STOCK) Act

It was passed by Congress and approved by President Obama in April 2012 is a good step in the direction. It restricts members of Congress from using any nonpublic information derived from the individual's position or gained from performance of the individual's duties, for personal benefit. Politicians are also required to report any purchase or sale of a security over $1,000 within 45 days. It includes a variety of other restrictions aimed and limiting insider trading in Washington, D.C.

6. Landmark cases

Much of the development of insider trading law has resulted from court decisions. A few of the landmark cases are discussed below: -

SEC v. Texas Gulf Sulphur Co.

Officers of the Texas Gulf Sulphur Corporation had used inside information about the discovery of the Kidd Mine to make profits by buying shares and call options on company stock. The court stated that anyone in possession of inside information must either disclose the information or refrain from trading.

Strong v. Repide, 1909

The Supreme Court of the United States ruled that a director who expects to act in a way that affects the value of shares cannot use that knowledge to acquire shares from those who do not know of the expected action.

Dirks v. Securities and Exchange Commission, 1984

This was a landmark case in insider trading based on tipping and defined what was termed as constructive insiders.

The Supreme Court of the United States ruled that tippees (receivers of second-hand information) are liable if they had reason to believe that the tipper had breached a fiduciary duty in disclosing confidential information and the tipper received any personal benefit from the disclosure.

In *Dirks*, the tippee received confidential information from an insider, a former employee of a company. The reason the insider disclosed the information to the tippee, and the reason the tippee disclosed the information to third parties, was to blow the whistle on massive fraud at the company. As a result of the tippee's efforts the fraud was uncovered, and the company went into bankruptcy. But, while the tippee had given the inside information to clients who made profits from the information, the U.S. Supreme Court ruled that the tippee could not be held liable under the federal securities laws, because the insider from whom he received the information was not releasing the information for a personal benefit but for the purpose of exposing the fraud. The Supreme Court ruled that the tippee could not have been aiding and abetting a securities law violation committed by the insider.

In *Dirks*, the Supreme Court also defined the concept of **constructive insiders**, who are lawyers, investment bankers and others who receive confidential information from a corporation while providing services to the corporation. Constructive insiders are also liable for insider trading violations if the corporation expects the information to remain confidential, since they acquire the fiduciary duties of the true insider.

SEC vs. Materia, 1984

This case expanded insider trading liability further as it first introduced the misappropriation theory of liability for insider trading. Materia, a financial printing firm proofreader, not an insider by any definition, was found to have determined the identity of takeover targets based on proofreading tender offer documents during his employment. After a two-week trial, the district court found him liable for insider trading, and the Second Circuit Court of Appeals affirmed holding that the theft of information from an employer, and the use of that information to purchase or sell securities in another entity, constituted a fraud in connection with the purchase or sale of a securities. The misappropriation theory of insider trading was born, and liability further expanded to encompass a larger group of outsiders.

United States v. Carpenter, 1986

This was a high profile case upholding mail and wire fraud convictions. It drew parallel from a prior ruling for a defendant who received his information from a journalist rather than from the company itself. The journalist R. Foster Winans was also convicted, on the grounds that he had misappropriated information belonging to his employer, the Wall Street Journal. The Court ruled that a person who acquires special knowledge or information by virtue of a confidential or fiduciary relationship with another is not free to exploit that knowledge or information for his own personal benefit but must account to his principal for any profits derived therefrom.

United States v. O'Hagan, 1997

The U.S. Supreme Court adopted the misappropriation theory of insider trading in this case. O'Hagan was a partner in a law firm representing Grand Metropolitan, while it was considering a tender offer for Pillsbury Company. O'Hagan used this inside information by buying call options on Pillsbury stock, resulting in profits of over $4.3 million. O'Hagan claimed that neither he nor his firm owed a fiduciary duty to Pillsbury, so he did not commit fraud by purchasing Pillsbury options. The court rejected his argument by explaining the misappropriation theory and recognizing a company's information as its property to which it has a right of exclusively use. O' Hagan trades were a deception of those who entrusted him with access to confidential information.

United States v. Newman, 2014

The United States Court of Appeals for the Second Circuit cited the Supreme Court's decision in *Dirks*, and ruled that in order for a "tippee" (a person who has received insider information from an insider and has used that information) to be guilty of insider trading, the tippee must have been aware not only that the information was insider information, but must also have been aware that the insider released the information for an improper purpose (such as a personal benefit). The Court concluded that the insider's breach of a fiduciary duty not to release confidential information—in the absence of an improper purpose on the part of the insider—is not enough for criminal liability to be imposed on the either the insider or the tippee.

These cases highlight how the ambit of rules around insider trading expanded over time with landmark rulings.

7. Recent insider trading cases

This section lists down few of the most surprising and sensational insider trading cases that came to light in the recent past with reasons that made them worth mentioning. In the second half, we discuss the Gammon hedge fund case in a little more detail.

Gammon hedge Fund – Raj Rajaratnam

It is the recent biggest hedge fund insider trading scam in the US. In this $45MN Galleon hedge fund scam by billionaire financier Raj Rajaratnam, he has been accused of carrying on a conspiracy for over three years since January 2006 along with two Indians at the Intel Capital treasury department. For the first time in the history of Wall Street insider trading case, Raj was accused of using telephone wire taps to share trading tips and make profits. Rajaratnam profited from information received from: Robert Moffat, a senior executive of IBM, considered next in line to be CEO, Anil Kumar, a senior executive of McKinsey & Company, Rajiv Goel, a midlevel Intel Capital executive, Roomy Khan, previously convicted of wire fraud for providing inside information from her employer, Intel, to Rajaratnam. Rajaratnam also conspired to get confidential information on the $5 billion purchase by Warren Buffett's Berkshire Hathaway of Goldman preferred stock prior to the September 2008 public announcement of that transaction. The Wall Street Journal reported that a former member of the board of directors of Goldman Sachs and former McKinsey & Company chief executive Rajat Gupta told Rajaratnam about Berkshire's investment before it became public. Gupta stood to profit as would-be chairman of Galleon International, a co-founder of New Silk Route with Rajaratnam, and as a friend of Rajaratnam. In March 2011 Gupta was charged in an administrative proceeding by the SEC. Gupta maintained his innocence, counter-sued, and won dismissal of the administrative charge, but was then arrested on criminal charges.

On May 11, 2011, Rajaratnam was found guilty on all 14 counts of conspiracy and securities fraud. And in October, was sentenced to 11 years in prison by Judge Richard Holwell. To date, this is the longest prison sentence ever handed out for insider trading. The thirteen other defendants connected to Rajaratnam's case received prison sentences averaging approximately three years each.

Martha Stewart, 2001

One of the most sensational inside trading scams till today is of TV tycoon Martha Stewart who was accused of receiving insider information and selling shares of ImClone drug just a day before the US Food and Drug Administration (FDA) denied approval for the drug.

Enron, 2004

The insider trading case of Enron took four years for the Justice Department to trace. This trading wiped out its employees' retirement accounts and stunned investors. The company's former CEO Jeff Skilling made an $89MN profit allegedly from the sale of artificially inflated Enron stocks and options.

8. Should insider trading be legal?

We have discussed above why insider trading should be illegal. But some economists and legal scholars such as Henry Manne, Milton Friedman, Thomas Sowell, Daniel Fischel, and Frank H. Easterbrook have argued that laws against insider trading should be repealed. They claim that insider trading based on material nonpublic information benefits investors, in general, by more quickly introducing new information into the market. Their arguments can be summarized as follows:-

- Insider trading brings more accurate information to the market through people most knowledgeable about deficiencies of the company. Trades by insiders are clearer indicators on the health of the company than other printed and publicly released information.

- Some argue that insider trading is a victimless act. A willing buyer and a willing seller agree to trade property which the seller rightfully owns.

- Legalization advocates question why trading where one party has more information than the other is legal in other markets, such as real estate, but not in the stock market. For example, if a reputed builder through his politician friend knows of an upcoming government development plans in an area and buys property a good bargain from the seller, it is legal. But other arguments in favor state that in the case of a company, its shareholders are also owners and have an equal right to information. The leadership is liable to share that information with them.

- Some also propose legalizing insider trading on negative information which is often withheld from the market as trading on such information has a higher value for the market than trading on positive information.

- Data on legal insider trading is freely available on trading sites and can be analyzed. Traders taking cues from such trades usually benefit more than the rest who are ignorant to such information. It is thus argued, that such retail investors loose because of ignorance and would otherwise also not make use of the information available.

But opponents argue that insider selling is trickier. Insiders use restricted stock and options to supplement or, in some cases, virtually replace standard paychecks, so using this data to determine when to sell is less exact. When insiders are buying their own stock, they do so because they believe the stock is going up. When they sell, however, they could be doing so for a number of reasons like making investments and not simply because they believe that the share value may drop.

- Technical analysts point out that most insiders are investors, not traders and they tend to buy shares in the company when they are cheap and sell when they are expensive. They are not as motivated by trends as are traders. Insider transactions have proven to be a better buy than sell indicator.
- There is little doubt that as a sentiment indicator, insider buying and selling can be an effective trade confirmation tool when used in conjunction with other technical indicators such as trend lines and moving average crossovers by those who know how to read the signs.

9. Steps to check insider trading

Researchers have suggested and discussed ways in which insider trading can be curbed. Some of the most widely discussed ways are listed below:

- Preventing insiders from selling or buying stock in their company to once a quarter or 4 times a year. This would cause executives to signal their bullishness or bearishness on their company very clearly to investors.
- Public companies need to reduce the number of employees who are privy to non-public material information. They must also ensure that the people who do have access to this information clearly understand what insider trading consists of.
- Information theft must be checked by companies with investment in data protection systems.
- Employees must be made aware of what constitutes as insider trading and its legal ramifications.
- The size of the Federal Government could be reduced so that fewer people have access to this information thereby reducing the risk of insider trading.
- Increase federal sentencing guidelines. But this would be effective only if judges use them to their fullest extent. Many judges in the recent past have issued stiff monetary fines for insider trading, but the associated prison terms were relatively lax.

10. Conclusion

As markets and market participants grow, the risk of insider trading has also been growing. With information flowing faster than ever, there is limited control on its access and flow. This makes it difficult to both check and track insider trading. Companies therefore assume an even greater role to invest in systems, processes, trainings to prevent insider trading. Though governments have taken more and more stringent steps over time to prevent insider trading, it is important for economies to set global standards for insider trading so that it is easier to track it and prove it. Though people have prosecuted and punished for practicing insider trading, the greed for quick money exists. The cases for insider trading have been increasing with ever increasing uncertainty in the markets. This makes it all the more important to know about insider trading and educate employees about it.

11. References

1. https://www.measuringworth.com/ukcompare/relativevalue.php?use%5B%5D=CPI&use%5B%5D=NOMINALEARN&year_late=1995&typeamount=1&amount=1&year_source=1995&year_result=2016
2. http://www.telegraph.co.uk/finance/newsbysector/banksandfinance/11425522/Twenty-years-on-is-Nick-Leeson-really-sorry-for-breaking-the-bank.html
3. https://www.sec.gov/rules/final/33-7881.htm
4. https://www.bloomberg.com/view/articles/2015-02-12/insider-trading-on-tender-offers-is-still-illegal
5. http://www.investopedia.com/terms/i/insidertrading.asp
6. https://www.sec.gov/fast-answers
7. https://en.wikipedia.org/wiki/Raj_Rajaratnam#Conviction_and_imprisonment_for_insider_trading
8. http://www.nytimes.com/topic/person/raj-rajaratnam
9. http://www.cato.org/pub_display.php?pub_id=12724

ISBN 9781535415064

90000 >